THE STRIPED WORLD

The Striped World EMMA JONES

faber and faber

First published in 2009
by Faber and Faber Limited
3 Queen Square London WC1N 3AU

Typeset by Faber and Faber Limited
Printed in England by T. J. International Ltd, Padstow, Cornwall

A CIP record for this book
is available from the British Library

ISBN 978–0–571–24538–3

10 9 8 7 6 5 4 3 2 1

In memory of

Maureen Jones
1950–2007

'She can feel no stir
of joy when her girl sings'

★

The Suns Light when he unfolds it
Depends on the Organ that beholds it.

– WILLIAM BLAKE, *The Gates of Paradise*

Acknowledgements

Some of the poems in this book appeared previously in *Poetry London, The Rialto, The Warwick Review* and in *New Poetries IV* (Carcanet Press), and in anthologies from Rockingham Press and Middlesex University Press; I am grateful to the editors of these publications. Grateful thanks are also owed to the Master and Fellows of St John's College, Cambridge, for the award of a Harper-Wood Studentship in English Poetry and Literature; to the Varuna Writer's Centre, NSW; and to the Arts Council of Australia for an emerging writer's new work grant. My debts are many, but I am particularly grateful to my editor Matthew Hollis for scrupulous reading; to my father Graeme Jones; to Jean Jones, Greg Jones, Lynley Everest, Michael Jones, Amy Jones, Tommy and Sue Scully, and Donald Slattery; to Tracy Bohan; Micky Pinkerton; Heather Glen; Jennifer Barron; and to friends who have been generous readers, especially Jacob Polley, Sarah Hall, Greg McLaren, Sean Pryor, Judith Beveridge, Angela Leighton, and most particularly, Fiona McFarlane.

Contents

Waking

Here it is again, light hoisting its terrible bells.
As though a world might wake up with it –

The moon shuts its eye. Down in the street
the same trolley is playing the pavestones.

For twenty-five years I've been waking
this way. There was one morning

when my mother woke and felt a twitch
inside, like the shifting of curtains.

She woke and so did I. I was like a bird
beating. She had no time for anaesthetic.

We just rolled from each other like indecent genies.
Even the nurses were startled.

Now she says the world and I were eager
from the start. But I was only waking.

Farming

The pearls were empire animals.
They'd been shucked from the heart of their grey mothers
which is why, so often, you'll find them
nestled at the neck and breast.
It stood to reason.
The sea was one long necklace,
and they often thought of that country.

Its customs waylaid them,
and it occupied their minds.
Nobody missed them.
The oysters felt nothing,
neither here nor there,
down on the farm and miles out to sea,
those swaying crops.

Rolled to create circumference.
Opened to accommodate
the small strange foreign irritant
that hones itself to a moon.
The oysters say
'it's a lulling stone, that outside heart
turned in, and beating.'

They knit their fields of nacre, and are quiet.
The clouds converge.
It's a sad constabulary,
the sky and the sea, and the boats.
Because piracy is common
the farmers carry guns. Does the sea
object, marshalling its edges?

Do the fish know
their glint, those inward birds
in the fields of the Pacific?
It's a singing bone,
the indivisible pearl.
It's a bright barred thing. And pearls
are empire animals. And poems are pearls.

Tiger in the Menagerie

No one could say how the tiger got into the menagerie.
It was too flash, too blue,
too much like the painting of a tiger.

At night the bars of the cage and the stripes of the tiger
looked into each other so long
that when it was time for those eyes to rock shut

the bars were the lashes of the stripes
the stripes were the lashes of the bars

and they walked together in their dreams so long
through the long colonnade
that shed its fretwork to the Indian main

that when the sun rose they'd gone and the tiger was
one clear orange eye that walked into the menagerie.

No one could say how the tiger got out in the menagerie.
It was too bright, too bare.
If the menagerie could, it would say 'tiger'.

If the aviary could, it would lock its door.
Its heart began to beat in rows of rising birds
when the tiger came inside to wait.

Zoos for the Living
(a ballad)

I

And then I saw the drowned town of Adaminaby.
Colonial postcard! The town still stands (terra nullius).
It was founded by blue-eyed imperial apes. They soothed
its river, and diverted it like an infant. And they erected
a dam, to carefully drown a suave and mythical valley.

Here they flustered a republic of bright and singular birds.
(For, on the banks of the Snowy, the avid ornithologist
can find numerous examples of flat-skulled horn-beaked
parrots, in various shades, chewing their grey babel tongues;
and a religious-minded bird there might cry out and stand,

flexing its bright crest, and look to heaven like a hot crowned man,
like an amorous punk, King David in a promised land,
and cry to that river 'O Absalom!'). When it shut,
the Snowy River on Adaminaby, most of the town
had already moved, in convoys, brick by brick,

like that agile forest in *Macbeth*, to new Adaminaby.
And they raised its stones like the bones of Christ.
And they combed out its roads like dusty, long, messianic hair.
And they found it to be good. Arthur Yen had been landlord there,
old Chinese stock. He was birthed in a gold rush pan.

And rubbed shoulders with Leicke and Lominici and Laszlo.
And of course with Charles McKeahnie, the Man from Snowy River,
who tethered his horse to the beer-pump, while the bargirls
foamed and wept. And what's left of old Adaminaby?
New Adaminaby. Old and new Adams. And the steps

of St Mary's Church, and one pillar, that burdens the river
with an absent bell and the toll of a nautical angelus.
And fishermen farm the once-lived-in streets, angling their lights.
And these are streetlamps for the dead. And the dead once made
Adaminaby. And the General Store once stocked their wares.

II

Where I live now, there's an afternoon storm. This is February.
There are mountains, blue, with humid birds. It's summer here.
And my mother was 'a ten-pound pom'. Her fine, pale, English,
cigarette-paper skin was frail, untouched by the sun or the Mersey,
was nourished in Ireland, imported by famine and the nineteenth
    century

to an England of docks and of ships, where Our Lady of Hunger
smoked on the steps of the barred yard, and dragged the grey tides,
and where my great-great-aunt the money-lender tied her one son
to the bed, to keep him from sailing to Sydney, Australia,
where his father stood by the harbour, and watched it breathe.

And so my mother took the plane instead. A beebop blonde
blue-eyed British jitterbug, she had a ticket to ride.
And her skin was as pale as the lashed cliffs at Dover.
It had a quality. It had a ring to it. And I was stitched in:
an alleged convict-celt, with a bland façade

like an Anglican chapel, and with secularized, mild,
deferential, careful, middle-class good manners.
And as a kid I loved the old-style ballads, the plaints
of the convict Irish, and patriotic doggerel,
and rhyming prayers. And blood's a tied and sleepy boy.

[6]

And – skin recedes. There are swaying towns, just covered.
And oil flaps in the water, and the blue and white water
turns yellow; and sickness lulls her nacreous town; and the rains
draw back, and the rains draw back; and drought comes,
not an absence, but a thing; and nothing is necessary.

And old Adaminaby asserts itself. The steps of the church
assert themselves; they step to the blank air; in a curved world
they look to heaven. And now drought undoes the flood, and dry things
glitter; the roads refasten like bones in a ballad; the buildings shift
in their absent bricks; and chimneys ride the air like flutes.

And things happen in Adaminaby. And it's not empty.
And a wind carries birds. And 'the ring-neck parrots
are a cloud of wings, and the shell-parrots are a cloud
of wings', and water is a host, and fire is a host.
They mother things. They're clever ghosts, and blessèd among women.

Subcontinental Postcard

When the sun, that gradual sepoy
rose, then clouds occurred;
the sea came, and hung like a man;
the tankers boiled,
and a wind rifled the trees.

The day was still far off,
and filled with mercantile buildings.
Everyone's deaths
sat in the margins.
On the edge of things,

things swayed;
the lobster-pots and the crab-pots;
the antediluvian
aircraft of the insects;
and the sea that wrote in a fine crabbed hand.

Goldfish

The sea's not wide but it is full.
I have my castle and my load of gold.
See how the chest flips up to show
its plastic pennies and its bouldered hearts
with each great current, while in droves
we follow close the circular turret –

The sea's not wide but it is full.

Daphne

And if I was changed, what was the difference?
And if I was strung – myself and not myself,
a double thing, there was a consequence.
When I was a girl, I was a girl.
And now I'm a tree, I'm a tree.

Seasons don't arrive. There's just a shifting.
We move. I see it now. The staid worlds move,
and the sun is no dragged lamp. The gods die,
or never lived. They crawl home, damp and slow,
to the subtle, shallow sea that made them.

I'm not that happy. It's not important.
And I'm not sad. It's good to be a girl,
and a tree, with the wind in it. It's good
to move in the wind, and to move the wind.
My leaves all move. They sing, and make the world.

Painting

Everyone's souls, which didn't exist, were playing up,
and they flocked as the shadows we left on the ground
when the tired sun – that midday man – was an artist.
And they surfaced in our sweat, which made, for us,
a soft and lunar garment worn abroad; an outline,
and a second skin. The inside out, the outside in –

And still the light comes, and into the eye,
and with it a world, and a borderland.
And you set your easel between the rocks
and you painted the way a man might paint
if he weren't a man, but a dismal bird
who saw below him stretched a dismal bird-
land, filled with wind, and white paper,
and made of beautiful, counterfeit birds –

Such glyphs, such strokes,
the gathered arabic
of themselves, their wings,
those folded homes
as each dull sail,
dull soul, takes off.

And you said 'every memory's a motel.'
Dull soul, dull sail.
And death was a breezy man who arranged
and rearranged the birds and branches and
'can the clouds continue until evening?'
you said, perched upon the classical rocks,
apish and pale, claw-footed, like a bath.

Then the canvas said 'there's no division,
just a vision forced of earth and sky.'
But the painting leaned out, forgetful,
and made the day in its own image.

Window

His sadness was double,
it had two edges.

One looked out –
onto skylines,
and streets with ice-cream
men, and cars,
and clouds
like cut cotton.

The other stayed in
to watch
his memories unbuckle
and his hairs
all repeat
in the washstand.

Both were impatient.
Sometimes they'd meet
and make a window.

'Look at the world!' said the glass.
'Look at the glass!' said the world.

The Mind

flares out –

as though it held a separate existence,
as though it were
a kind of massy paradise
closer to God than the venal organs –

electric marmoset,
diminutive earl –

here are your subjects and your penal inhabitants,
your cracked and cleaving citizenry.

Worldly, you cling: I live in you like a paradisal ape
lives in a garden, walled, with onlookers;
as the zookeeper lives; as the girl lived in that house.

Conversation

'Oh this and that. But for various reasons' –
(the season, and the change in season, the season of grief

and retrospection, the rooftop pulled from the childhood
house, and the internal doll in its stuck seat,

that is, the fictive soul in its brute cathedral, and because of memory,
maybe, and organs in niches, and the beat to things,

and the knowledge that the body is the soul and vice versa,
but that false distinctions are sometimes meaningful,

and that difference, all difference, is just distance, not a state,
not a nation, and because nothing *matters*, not really,

or everything does, I don't mind being an animal, at all,
because a sentient thing is nothing else, and because toward matter

I feel neither love nor hate but the kind of shuttered
Swiss neutrality a watch might feel for time

if it had an animal's sentiments, knowing itself a symbol
and function, knowing itself a tool, and because I feel

the dull culmination of various phenomena informing me
and am that culmination, I feel ill in some small way,

though not ill really, just idle, and I prefer, you see,
to keep an impassive inviolable pact with things that tick,

with solitary, shifted things, and because my life's approximate act
is the sister to some other life, with different tints, I carry

and nurse, my diffident twin, I'm often morose, and think
of those statues that lean above themselves in water,

those fountains, stone, with commemorative light,
with disfiguring winds, and because reflection is an end in itself

and because there's an end even to reflection, and an end to the eye,
that heated room, I prefer to keep my artifice and my arsenal

suspended, close; like an angled man; like the stationed sun;
and because matter ends, or I should say, matter turns to matter,

and my small inalienable witness to this is real, I can't pretend
to wish to be a rooted thing, full-grown, concerned

with practical matters, in a rooted world, and careful of borders,
when an ineradicable small portion glints, my mind, that alma mater,

and says, make your work your vicarage) – 'I put off going back'.

Equator

On the old ships,
when they crossed the line,
the Captain became cabin boy
and the cabin boy
'Neptune, King of the Brine!'

In curls and rouge
they'd play at this,
a contrary crew. Then the last bell rang;
the boy resigned;
and the Captain resumed his place.

He wrote in the log:
'Today, on course,
we crossed the line, with usual incident.'
And he also wrote:
'There is no line.'

Hush

No one in the city.
No one and nothing.
No one walks down the long colonnades
or stops to look in a window
or waits in groups at pedestrian crossings.

No one in the city.
Nothing and no one.
Empty cars. Empty beds.
The city has a lullaby and it's hatched,
walking through the streets, saying 'shhh.'

Things glitter on trays in the empty hospital.
An isolate city. No one mans
the balloon stands and feeds the zoo animals.
The city looks to the harbour,
but it doesn't want to be submerged.

It doesn't want a porpoise to fly past
the office window and its rows
of copy machines. It doesn't want,
it doesn't want. It doesn't want to think to say
'road', 'roof', 'parking meter', 'bird'.

Winnowing

It was a definite change, a migration.
It was a paring down to something lone and lashless –
autumn, a lunar season.
It moved through the traffic,
and ate early dinners in the restaurants,
and got shorter in the afternoons.
It was like someone who saw themselves
in the mirror and got sad;
who grew their hair long, then cut it off.

The trees were blatant, letting themselves go,
leaving dull eyes spread in the gutters.
And a builder had left a radio in the rubble,
and the music moved, and the wind got a song in its head
and couldn't forget it, till the wind *was* the song,
and the wind was just something the song
had known once, and the song was worried by the gust
it felt, sometimes, inside, moving it along,
a white wave, a moving thing.

It was part of a philosophy:
things on top of other things
the city with its greenery
and the offices built of paper
and the harbour that holds its own shelved city
with the living
drowned in the boats of their collarbones.

Walk out a little and on the edge of the city
there are green half-fields, and buildings
in a shuttered sleep, and gathering animals.

Where one thing, there, becomes another –

(Or, just give in to it, the problem –
the coloured, colouring thing –
Newspaper report: different country, country scene.
Twenty years on, windy field, exhuming the bodies,
mass grave, trench number three: the bones
of a foetus in the bones of a woman:
'tiny bones, femurs, thighbones the size
of a matchstick.'
                    Spread babushka –
rainy season, 'the time for winnowing'.
Drowsy season. The bombs grow like blue flowers.)

Sperm Song
(a shanty)

Where was I, my darling, when that moon
came in, a paper cut Cupid,
to stupidly loll its white eye?

It's a raucous knuckle, blind as a bat.
What's that? What's that?
Shot comets, here. Constellations, here.
Where was I, when the moon came in?

I was boring great tunnels in the Andes (heigh ho)
I was lifting the lid of the oceans (ditto)
I was in the heated part of the bed, the centre of the world.

Cities flew from me on fabulous stalks.

Where was the moon in all this?

I'll shatter that bead of the moon.

Creator

I felt, with a pang, a second self
rear its glossy spreading head,
and I thought, is there a snake in my yard?

It fed daily and nightly. I winced
warm coins into its mouth,
and changed my arrangements.

But nothing could please it for more than an hour.
Soon it was
estranged from nearly all its relations.

Still, there are times when it will climb to my lap
and try to make up.
It looks up to me, it raises its face,

and I'm reminded then
of the natural mirror
that can assert itself, at certain times:

unruffled sky,
unruffled lake,
their same slung clouds.

And if it's mistaken me for someone else,
a shaky god
with its own plain face on

then that's no problem, either.
This is just
its funny condition.

What I couldn't forgive, if I knew or cared,
is its subtle
and wilful predator's

refusal to make proper provision
for itself and its young.
This is dullness.

Or its dull belief in our separation –
as though it could
exist without me! As though

it could proclaim its independence!
There's no scope
there, for civilized neutrality.

A case in point:
because it thinks we're different,
it named me.

This was the turning
point in our relationship.
It named me,

as though I were one thing.
One thing, merely!
One thing, to be one thing –

As though constancy was general.
As though I was a separate matter.
As though I were quite serious.

Even now, if it looked
in the parted
portions of the wall

where the room
makes the room again
in dull reverse

or leans to the skinny rim
of its harboured glass
to view the rubbished garden

then still, we'd be facing each other.
And still it would say:
here's my portion.

See it there, looking up,
its raised face
struck like a clock's?

What does it want? There, there.
I'll let it go. If a mother knows,
if a mother cares, she forgets these things.

A Literary History

Candles – why wave your hands about that way?
    Your wicks throw out inappropriate shadows.
    You can't be gothic before gothic *was*
        you know, and Mary Wollstonecraft
        hasn't given birth to Mary Shelley yet.

Not quite. There are two more minutes. The eigh-
    teenth century has a cough and Mary Senior
    is slack and all shifty in the bed with its
        half-expired shawls and its literary sweat
        where she's lain, she feels, for a thousand years

till, two minutes up, Mary Junior shows just her face,
    a wet homunculus, and Frankenstein's monster
    hides under the bed, and Mary Senior dies
        two-headed (death hasn't read
        'A Vindication on the Rights of Woman')

and Percy Bysshe Shelley, still a boy, dreams with the face
    of a drowned man of the Campo dei Fiori,
    where, just then, someone wakes up, and stands,
        and lights a candle to the Virgin Mary, whose
        'mystical rose' coughed the Word up like a pearl.

Pietà

Baby, you sure look sick.
When I first held you that's what I thought,
this one won't last.

Everyone wanted a piece of you.
But I held you close, and the sky leaned in
all filled with rain, and those first-time

singers cleared their throats,
their hair all in the tops of trees and the motel signs.
See, I said, I've seen a sign!

and we pulled up on the escarpment
and ate fried food, and you took your breaths
in droplets, and drank so deep the streetlights spun with milk.

By morning you were thirty.
So gassed and shaken. A wind had caught itself
in you and couldn't get out.

Hey, I said, don't snag on his insides,
they're all he's got. But your heart shook like a guitar
that gets played and played

and only knows those songs,
the sorrow songs,
and you said 'sing to me'

and baby, I like to sing, so off we went,
and sang 'Love in the Museum'.
That's a good one, though it makes me cry.

See, I said, there's love in the museum!
I straightened out your fingers one by one.
You died, and your face stayed on the sheets.

I was restless then. I hate those nights.
You're heavy, baby.
The weight of a man in your bones.

Why you want the face of a man
with the face of a child?
Why have one and still the other?

You're small for a man. That's what they say.
They look at me funny.
Every eye naked as a highway

of bathers stretched by the pools on the motel roofs,
every one the same, one after the other,
while we looked for a place to lay our heads.

You sleepy now. I have a thing in me.
A bird or something.
It's cold, and knows the words of songs.

We sing now. Baby? You there?
I'm tired. I've seen your breath, flagged man.
You going now. Should we go. Baby?

Tenants

That beast in the laburnum, that lion in the bee
has something to do with industry.
All day he packs his savannah into cases,
for his Jerusalem.

Honey, drudge, the sun has shown
a flagellant's ease above the factory stacks.
Its only knowledge is practical smoke.
What a tutelary gun.

And here's a tenanted place on the border of nothing.
And on the nothingness, fields, with houses;
and in the houses, beasts; nothing spun;
and a promised land.

Waiting

The rain perturbs the panes. Only the wind
which has shuttled
through the stained and solid brick of the library tower

has brought some words from your future books
through the window's crack
to deliver you now, with its printed birds.

Here are words, and here's that sea, waiting.
The cold and mackerel-cracked
Atlantic that shakes from the lip of a mussel-shell.

It says 'why write? there's nothing in it.'
When we were girls
we had the souls of girls

and now that we've grown
we have the souls of girls. Why say
'innocence ends' when the same

blue bird beats in the chest
as before, and we breathe the same blue water?
I haven't put childish things from me.

And when I spoke as a child
there was no difference. So should they write
'innocence ends', or 'there's no such thing'?

And should you write? Wind, white cloud,
white paper. White swan
on water the colour of macadam,

thin brown river writing the swan.
Is there ever an end to comparison?
I miss, for example, the sub-tropical

light through stained glass, a world
contained in each hot pane,
a red or green or pearl-world

poised like a cracked gardenia
strewing its level scents. And there was
a consequence to things –

the light moved, and the man in the window
walked down the stairs.
And we walked too,

through a hackneyed adolescence
of holidays, debates, class and coca-cola,
the terrible measure

of time the pinned tides in the hems
of our school skirts,
let down at the end of every summer.

You were certain of things,
you went to church.
And I was a surveyor

who noted carefully
a growing sense of desolation
in the topography

of foliage and of wincing traffic,
the blasted part of me
the bluest part, with its soft lashed lid.

We kidded round. The wind
snagged in us like terrible breath.
But it was beautiful too,

a desultory god in the suburbs
who floated on the backyard pools
trailing a hand in the water

and raising it like the back of a cat.
We were raised!
I was raised. Father, mother –

Father in the garden. Mother a pietà.
And then: the full light
winced to a little wick,

sunsets receded, fanned from the backs
of airplanes, the slow
stars replaced themselves

one by one, and the Southern Cross
moved to Orion. And you moved –
birds, rain, the cracked Atlantic

shifting its hydraulic soul
of muted oil, that spreading peacock.
Rustling and cold,

that sea is the feathery ink of Columbus.
Where's the green of the Pacific?
Those blank and burdened hills?

Boston. Salem. Massachusetts.
Hamburgers in pilgrim caps.
And in restaurants on the Cape

the droll shell of the scooped-out oyster.
The elaborate love rituals
of Mayflower descendants,

the little ship tacking in their blue blood,
as small as a ship on a sampler.
And where's the end of it?

New York Harbor? The Statue of Liberty
taking off like an ocean liner?
The blue *Titanic*? Moby Dick?

Or those flustered gulls the colour of money
that launder themselves on the sea-drifts
crying 'America! America!'

We're waiting, you say. It's clear –
the light above the rain,
the light below,

the window's shaky replica
and the way we hang
between two points

like strung-out Alices, or beating birds,
so pained, you say,
and so illuminated – waiting

for the words to come, the more real words –
like the skin with its hint
of a shipwreck, that might rise, sometime, to the top.

Gardener

A kind of anxious man
one day rose from the dead
and walked to the nearest town
where the women were playing bingo
and the TVs chorused quietly.

And he asked 'What happened?
What am I, and where have I been?'
One citizen could see he was honest,
and cleared the room above his garage,
and made this man his gardener.

All day now this man will sit
on a ride-on mower, in fictive America,
and groom the grass in rows,
and hear the cuttings rot,
and the bees blaze in the trees.

Sonnet

Here it is again, spring, 'the renewal'.
People have written about this before.
And the people who track the four seasons,
the hunters who know the weather has changed.

Still, rains happen; there are slow roots that make
progress; something has a hand in the earth
and turns it. Clouds unknot the wind. Bulbs blow.
Their threadbare minds gust outward, turn yellow

eyes to heaven. It answers with the sun.
And the sun is a bulb, a mutual bomb.
The daffodils crack. 'Oh heavens!' they fret,

'Where's your terminus?' The flowers are wan
travellers. They unpack their cases. All
they know, they are. Renewal, rest. Renewal.

Sentimental Public Man

I was a penitentiary.
A self-held
man, and bounded.

But when I stood up,
the world was righted,
and I saw the horizon just fine.

The sun rose there and bled.
It's got a rhythm.
I felt a dull commensurate beat in me,

and I said, what's that bird in a cage?
Who's that man?
My barred heart

saw the striped world turn like a beast
and said 'open yourself up,
son, and spread out for loving.'

So I wore my heart on my chest,
all decorative.
And it flared like the hair of a parrot.

That was my trademark.
They kissed it, the girls.
They died, and subsided.

Just a little bit, mind.
A pill in water
foams and subsides like the sun in water,

it spreads, and is rested.
Two in one,
a new thing.

What a blue union there is
between this wall and its shadow,
this open door and its held world.

Scenery's its thought.
It veers and is tilted; it swings from its roots.
My keeper unlocked it, a grave man.

I want to walk alone
on the city streets.
But is this permissible?

Someone walks with me for my protection.
And if I say
'things happen, and an average man

is made a brilliant thing
by solitary acts
and the gaze of his countrymen'

he says nothing;
it's as if his pocket mirror had spoken;
it's as if we must

as he says, go out, bright and blank,
and draw the world in,
and make it in our image.

Man, it was hard to turn thirty,
to feel my youth
thin to an alley, a kind

of pale propped girl on a garbage bin.
Such hunger, apprehension.
Such a handled thing.

But the buildings listened.
When they leaned in, it was like the day
leaned in with its lights on,

every window a wide eye.
The streetlamps listened,
and the businessmen, and the office workers.

I was a piece of work, ticking.
And my songs
were their measure of longing.

I said, well, take it.
Please take it away!
How good it would be, I thought, to be empty.

So I wiped myself out.
For days I lay, a gin-clear man,
a beaten man, of beaten glass.

A trammelled man.
And as though I were a path
lit for their use

the stars dwindled, losing sight,
the brain dwindled,
that cracked house,

and the overhead light
flared backward like a rearing girl,
and passed away.

Their love dismembered me.
As though my head lay
in the sea, my arms in the desert,

and the cool promontory
of my singing throat in the city streets.
My limbs gathered grass.

When will the end come,
and the chorus sing?

Baby, your arms feel sweet.
I remember them,
the subtle wheat of their pastures.

They've rocked me awake.
And I say, if this is life, if death is life,
then let me die

the way I died when I was born,
alone, with you. That straddled light.
And I also say: don't touch me.

Paradise

What you wanted was simple:
a house with a fence and a kind of gulled
light arching up from it to shake in the poplars
or some other brand of European tree
(or was it American?) you'd plant
just for the birds to nest in and so
the crows who'd settle there
could settle like pilgrims.

Darling, all day I've watched the garden make its way
down the road. It stops at the houses
where the lights are on and the hose reel is tidy
and climbs to the windows to look inside
like a child with its eyes of flared rhododendrons
and sunflowers that shutter the wind like bombs
so buttered and brave the sweet peas gallop
and the undergrowths fizz through the fences
and pause at some to shake into asters and weep.

The garden is a mythical beast and a pilgrim.
And when the houses stroll out it eats up
their papers and screens their evangelical dogs.

Barbecue eater,
yankee doodle,
if the garden should leave
where would we age
and park our poodle?

'This is paradise,' you said,
a young expansive American saint.
And widened your arms to take it in,
that suburb, spread, with seas in it.

Exhibit

On August 7, 1974,
Philippe Petit, high-wire artist,
who wishes to live very old,
took a bow and arrow and fishing line
and bridged the two towers
of the World Trade Center in New York.

He called it an artistic crime.
And onlookers said there was no wind
when he crossed the line, back and forth,
eight times or more. He just exhibited
the courage of those extraordinary steel workers,
who feel below them, swinging, vacant space.

Citizenship

In a room like this, with the sail of a ship
passed through the upper glass
of the doorway, and the walls lined with books,
Henry Kissinger: Years of Upheaval, and books on war presidents,
and elms in the windows, and the pilgrim dead
ballooned from their branches
like spinnakers winched to the dead Atlantic –
it's good to be an alien, in America.

I think so, today. The ship is a half-
sized replica
of another ship, the *Rose Dorothea*.
Or something. For reasons of atmosphere and commemoration
it lives here, in the municipal library,
looking out,
with the atmospheric, commemorative books,
to the matronly seaside.

Perspective fills the window. It flattens.
Litter takes to the streets.
The snow has loosed its mind. It was stiff
when it lived with us, and moored our doors, a kind of cool
and cradled patriarch. Law-bound.
It forced the town
to show its bones. I saw it on the doorsills,
I saw the white rafters.

The town was made again. Transformed.
Can I be transformed? Is it possible?
Or is transformation too constant? The snow
that goes on the road, the beat-up snow, that hitches

itself from town to town, and falls,
and subsides, and rises.
Ascension has a smell to it, ascension has a form,
when air hauls water.

Permanent change, the permanence of change.
In the window, the sky meets the sea,
its neutral twin in the wash-stand.
I like it, this town. This pilgrim ark, and its other half,
its pretty twin, the nice resort.
The sea today
a dolled-up policeman, and a citizenry,
patrolling nothing, patrolling.

Here, my sight is a wrecked president. An act.
I see, and I want to see
other things. The particular grit.
Rococo-less stars. I want to see particles, not pictures.
As though there could be matter without memory.
As though I wasn't
a visitor, in these parts, as though I wasn't
made, a limited thing.

Because I'm tired of fabulation. Not the pilgrim dead
in the trees, not death with its spinnaker,
no calamitous history moving there,
but a wind. Just a thin North American seasonal wind.
It was good to give myself time, it was good
to be an artefact
washed up and out on the timely rocks,
the buoys, of Massachusetts.

Here, even the omniscient man in the town clock's
a civil man; he says
'look out for time' as though it were

a ready thing; as though it were a plan,
not a process. These things, these processional things –
the wind makes the flag,
the sea makes the shore, they show how grave it is to be free.
Here's my face in the glass of the shelf.

Call me Rose Dorothea. I prefer the word
for the thing to the thing itself.
I'm bound by a kind of secular piety.
I lack. I'm like that man who came home from a trip one day
to find his funeral arranged, and a drowned man
misidentified
as himself. He tried to protest his life.
But they said, 'you're no citizen'.

Death's Sadness

Who knows death's sadness when he parts his hair?
He parted it to the right, then left.

Death was a sad Vatican, his own state.
His lookout was a little mirror.

He sure was clever. The buildings slid.
Death had a hand in that and everything.

Zoos for the Dead

From the late nineteenth century to the 1960s Australian governments, as
a practice and a policy, removed part-Aboriginal mothers, families and
communities, often by force. The children were placed in institutions. In
many cases physical mistreatment, sexual exploitation and extreme forms
of moral humiliation occurred. No one knows exactly how many children
were removed. – ROBERT MANNE

I have two things: a parrot, and a house by the water.
The first of these sits in a broken cage and looks with melancholy
attention at the second, which is stilted on the glitter

the sea and sky send out in gullish waves, wholly
engrossed with one another, an eye looking at an eye.
My parrot's name is Narcissus. He's the survivor of an atrocity.

He's the last in one long line. He is very serious. When I
was handed him in his faulty cage my friend said: 'remember,
no one knows what he knows, or the things that he's seen die.'

I considered this a bit dramatic, but believed it when his Goya-
etching face was first scooped from the gloom of his shirt-front
and angled me two white eyes winched on a lamé collar.

Sad in his drag, he'd sidle on blue legs looking for breakfast
at my pillow's edge, and say something in another tongue.
I'd write the word down in a special book. His language is important.

My language is official but his is important the way a medium
is when she speaks and the audience is one wide subsided
mouth. It's like a dream you remember, just before it goes again.

It's like the fall of Rome. It's irrevocable, and consecrated.
His previous owners were the last of their tribe. They were brother
and sister. The bird was their slow son. They followed

the rules of their lost nation and never spoke to one another
after his voice deepened and the wind dragged milk from her breasts.
They sat side by side like locked gardens. They tended one another.

One day they got a house for their painting and their parrot and
    their secrets.
They lived there very quietly. They spoke to the bird,
who kept their language. And when they died he came to me, in that
    way of parrots.

     ★

He hates flying, so I take his cage for walks. If he's quiet, and there's
    nothing
to record, we go for hours through the hairy dunes, to my old bay
and the wreck of the *Miranda*. On weekends there are things to
    watch: the floating

tourists; snorkellers in their sagged fluorescent suits, whole families
    of them, sipping day
through thin whistles; and ice-cream men, and divers in their lizard-
    skins.
Such scholarly mermen and mermaids –

> *The hardest thing, the first time, is to just go in.*

> On my first dives the deck would fly

backwards and the sun turn green. Then, when I'd see the currents
    send
shoals of slapped mackerel veering
from boats, I'd wince: I saw the sea had a mind

full of things and things, and now I was one of them, floating.
We were filled with filmy breath, we were death's trespassers.

> *how to stitch yourself to that dull soul-noise,*
> *inch by inch, in little waves.*

[46]

But we'd adjust. We did up our goggles. We found the wreck, squinting,

and we'd move above it like birds in slow circles, stung by some centre,
and find the loam of its beams, the twisted skins of its coins, and one bell
with a splayed case, that sidled its tongue like a worm on the currents,
    like bait for Narcissus.

We'd fiddle with our water torch. Here were fish and our empty tins.
    Here were fish and the pull
of the sea.
    It was a slack pearl, my stoppered-up mouth with its wide twin
    of two eyes in their plastic casing, two old-style pilots, small blue
        bombers.

                        Here was the ship in a rill of lichen.
We parted its shabby skirts. Smacked its itinerant world of fish –
                      No thin whistles kept us afloat.
                      We swung our wide lace feet.
                      Such a beautiful bombardment!
                      On our backs a tank of air,
                      the sky with its bird scrawl,
                      and the spread of the coastal town.
                                A wall

had formed around the ship's perimeter. Sand banks and the shackled
    clams. In
the hold, some chains – the sea's green anklet.
                    They caught, by chance, a mutineer who'd left
Tahiti. As a prisoner he was civil. We get the time of the storm from his
    stopped watch
and, from his bones, their coordinates.
                      There are lessons for Narcissus.

I tell him that *sea-caves are often green, and jellyfish are blue,*
and they move to the roofs of the caverns
like souls in a cathedral. Every single one of them just nosing to go!

They sting. We say to the learners: *leave off the strings of those bad balloons,*
those light live wires, those water lianas, that flotsam, that death with a little light in.
They'll play above you like actors. They'll hang like saints. You'll think the sun

is a white coin there for you to hide from. You'll think that it's your own white eye. It can
come, this drunkenness.

       So we keep to it, the wreck. It has its roof and walls.
It has its comforts.

          Let's keep to it, I say to the bird, *let's keep our bargain.*

But what I want from him is a word for a word.

            I tell him *the captain tries, but the ship smells*
its future. On his bottle there is a picture of a ship. Its wood is green.
It looks to the sea and the sea looks back. The ship is only temporary.
   In the sky, gulls

widen, clouds walk off, and the renovated wartime airplanes spend so long in their worn
circles that the afternoon sounds like an old man's dream. I say to the bird, *let's remember*
how it happened. He says nothing at all when I spread a blanket on the dunes, open

his cage and read from our guide 'Informational notes on the wreck of the *Miranda*,
transport ship, bound for the south of Australia, lost with all hands on February 9,
1805, in conditions of bad weather; experienced divers only.' He was all replica;

I was his cure. Day after day we read together.
            One day I began to embellish the contents.

The water was thick with currents of birds moving like fish.
The storm had struck their cages open.
Pigeons and squabs lost feathers and grew gills.
The parents of the dead were soon comforted to see
their children hanging round the prows of their fishing boats.
Nets got caught in their knotty hair.
All the free settlers were given ten square miles
of seaweed each, and all the convicts were emancipated.

One day I went further.

Driven by example, soon every ship in the empire sank.
Certain edicts gave rise to protocols in the commonwealth of the drowned.
All trading was exact. Eyes for eyes and teeth for teeth.
The empire sank with the ships.
The walls of coastal cities walked seaward.
Ants built nests in banks
and one diarist famously noted:
'undiscovered lands are undiscovered,
and where we have been, we are no longer.'

I say to Narcissus,
'look, we could have had a confederacy of seagulls,'
but he's quiet, looking for lice; he's seen a lot; he's a realist.

★

When Narcissus's mother was taken from her mother
they taught her to say

Tower of David,
Mystical Rose,
Ark of the Covenant,
Morning Star

Narcissus repeated. When her brother

died she said a word not even Narcissus knew, and did
all the forms, and lived for two more years, a cure for anthropologists.
A beautiful blue cure! She stood with her flared

[49]

heart bleating on her chest and her tears they caught in little cups
and analysed for misery's sperm; she did little death shows,
'it happened this way', 'here's how he fell', and ate her last supper

every night, her womb a small brown plate, and let crows
settle on her eyes like garments, crows on the line of the telegraph
pole, and Narcissus twitched (*so much waiting,* my friend wrote, *so*

much waiting. She paints. She talks. We join the dots.) Narcissus waits;
he's a delicate man-handler. I offer him my hand and he'll take my
   littlest
finger like a worm.

        Ark of the covenant, he might say, *mirror of justice, cause*
of our joy.

      For my notes I'm given certain information.

                       They took her to the desert.

They called her quadroon. Was this a type of moon? It had four
   phases.

                            Tower of ivory.

Virgin most powerful.

        There hadn't been any blood yet. She sometimes spoke
to her brother. They wore white smocks. At night words were passed
   like babies
down the cots. Some nights men came through the desert. They
   drove the flocks.
Something happened in her gown and a rose grew in the desert.
They took it away. The wind dragged milk from her breasts. *River of*
   milk,

small sucked pearl! Wide white river. So many faces hovered there
   and leaned like white
flowers to see themselves that her streaked brown mirror cracked.
   She could walk
a thousand miles and still be nowhere different. Once she left. She
   was washing plates.

White faces rose from the foam. She just walked out the door and
through the paddock
and onto a road. The sun was a conspirator. She'd heard that every road
leads to the coast.
She walked carefully. *When she was young they'd given her stories. This is
for safekeeping.*

She could tell no one. She could tell her own children.
They brought her back. Then she washed the plates.

*Keep them in places where no one will look. In the whorl of your ear or
your eye.*
Her brother was droving.
They paid him in liquor. At night they'd get him to show his scars, or
find them water, or stand
on just one leg for an hour at a time. They'd clap and he'd smile.
When they found each other, they'd walk for hours keeping

silence. Rules are the rules and these were their rules. Sometimes at night,
the Holy Ghost was a wind
in the trees. A white wave, a spread of cockatoos. It was like the sea
made its way down
the highway. *Let's leave when the waters thicken. Let's leave when the
storms come.* One day a kind

man might come in a beautiful ute. *She lay on the grass with beautiful
utility.* He wanted to learn
the old ways. *To paint is to take the sky in and twist it.* Together, they
crushed the stones,
spat, added water. He was pink and rough as rose. They pulled beer
from each other's long

throats. He was from the city. He gave her a bird. He wrote her a poem.
He said *no one*
rhymes anymore. She taught him to paint a new way. *Once they'd sent
her pencils and a book*

called 'Join the Dots'. They drank sweet sherry and taught the bird to
   speak. *Virgin of virgins,*

said Narcissus, *Spiritual Vessel, Revved-Up Engine, Star of the Sea.*
                                            Can I say what the bird speaks?
Sometimes they'd lay in the wreck of a beautiful Ford and watch
   what was setting in the west.
He said she was proof that once the world was Paradise.

                          We took an eye, she got a tooth.
                          We took a tooth, she got a bone.

Narcissus, here's a copy of the painting by the man who knew the
   girl who mothered you:

              A woman sits by a window, looking out.
              She looks as though she were thinking of nothing in particular.
              She looks as though she might die someday.
              In the air there's a bird, a kind of disastrous parrot.
              His wings are spread. He's looking right at her.
              In his mouth he's holding something.
              It could be a child or a word.

He keeps her words and we look for them like worms. He looks at me,
   bored harlequin.
He has a secret.

                  (See, this is what I've discovered about Narcissus.
Narcissus has no soul. He's a black box, a pocket mirror. He sits
in his rill, and takes me nowhere. I think that, when Narcissus

dreams, he's the captain of parrots, and the world is a parrot's
wing, spread, with an itch in it. He's empty. Even now he sits by the
   door
of his cage, his faulty cage, and sleeps with his eyes open, and feels it

widen to take in all that sky, and the sea, that green macaw.)

Painted Tigers

have the same look, of something surprised.
But, at the same time, not surprised at all –

A vacancy, over which the stripes ride,
in a fictive jungle, and ministered

by Delacroix, who heats the vacancy.
Or by whoever found the tiger in

my 1950s three-toned textbook
trees and drew it out.

This illustration needs no root.
Stripes create the tiger for the eye;

the gallery wall hosts melanin shadows;
I have a plastic tiger on my desk finds prey in nothing
but the vacancy of shuttered windows.

I saw a copy of a copy once.
It was a Chinese painting, post-war;
in it, the tiger stands on a mountain,

looking out. Snow threatens him. His stripes
bead and sag. In the distance, a grey town.

The caption reads: 'the tiger has something on his mind'.
And in the commentary the tiger

is 'the symbol of the muffled artist'.
In the sky, a Communist

Creator leans, bearded and delicate,
through stilled winds, and the tiger stands, present;

and resolutely absent, too, looking
out onto nothing but an absence of tigers.

Snow is a philosophy. It paints tigers.
And the tiger has nothing on its mind.

Coda

You've worn yourself out among wan things,
pills and paper, bloodless birds.
And you've worn yourself like a whimsical dress
every day, and put yourself on, and said
'here's a gathered thing'
to the bland clock of the bedroom mirror.

The commuter wind has a sympathy,
and the commuter sun,
who illuminates leaves like a monk.

You don't see things or people, you see space –
the winch between two branches. You live in
the winch between two branches. Something spoke,
you answered. And you don't know what, or when.